EASTER ICONS
COLORING BOOK

HOPE AND LIFE PRESS

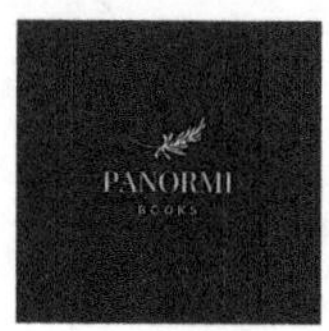

First published in 2019 by
PANORMI BOOKS

Easter Icons Coloring Book

Published by
PANORMI BOOKS
panormibooks.com

Printed in the United States of America.

CONTENTS

EASTER ICONS COLORING BOOK

Jesus Christ	5
Christ the Rabbi	6
The Mandylion	7
Do Not Weep For Me, Mother	8
The Transfiguration	9
Christ in Canaan	10
Christ and the Blind Man	11
Christ and the Apostles	12
Seven Loaves and Two Fishes	13
Christ the Good Shepherd	14
Christ and the Gerasene	15
Christ and Jairus	16
Christ and the Hemorrhaging Woman	17
Christ Healing	18
Christ with the Children	19
Christ and the Apostle Thomas	20
The Last Supper	21
The Holy Trinity	22
The Crucifixion	23
The Resurrection	24

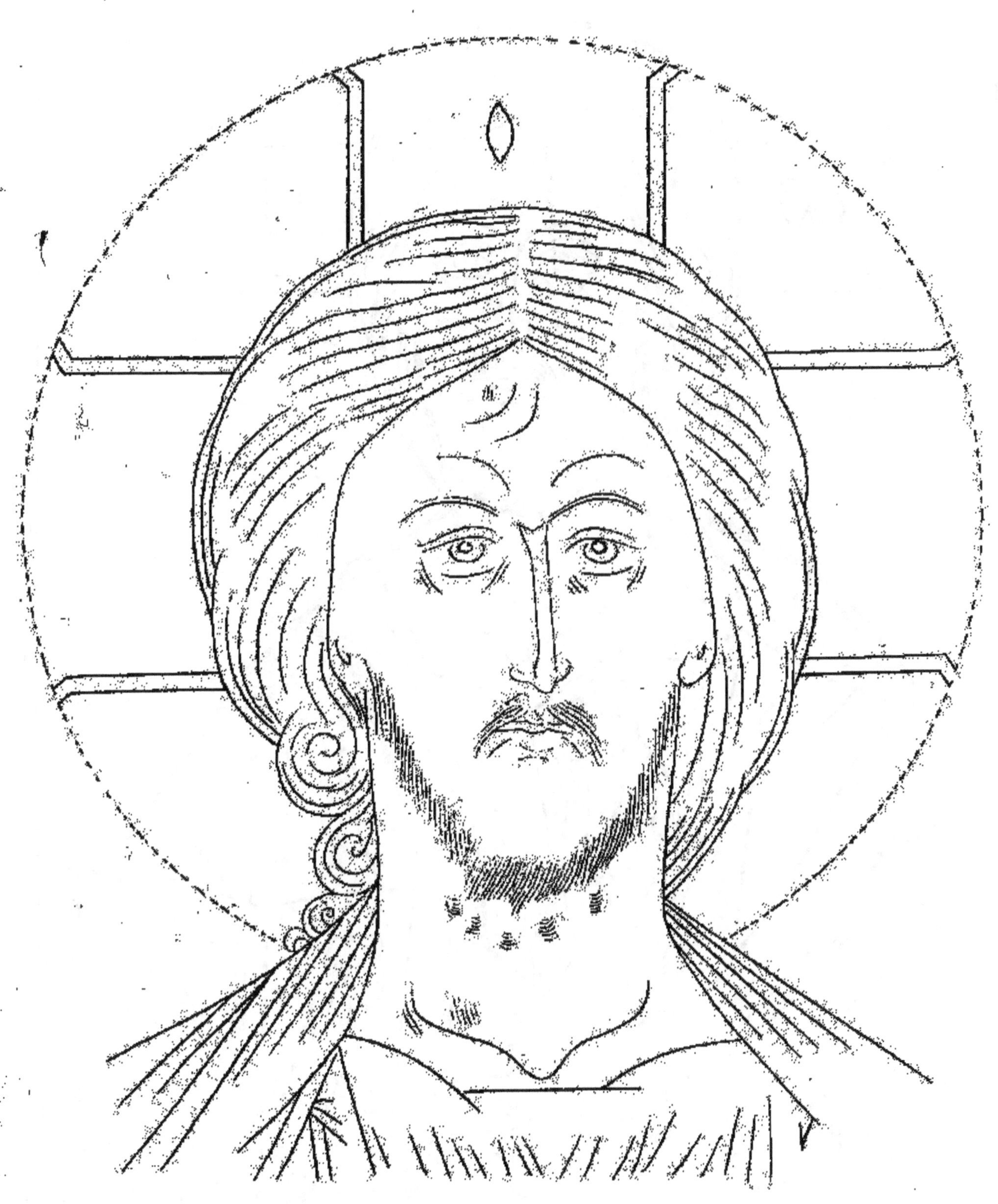

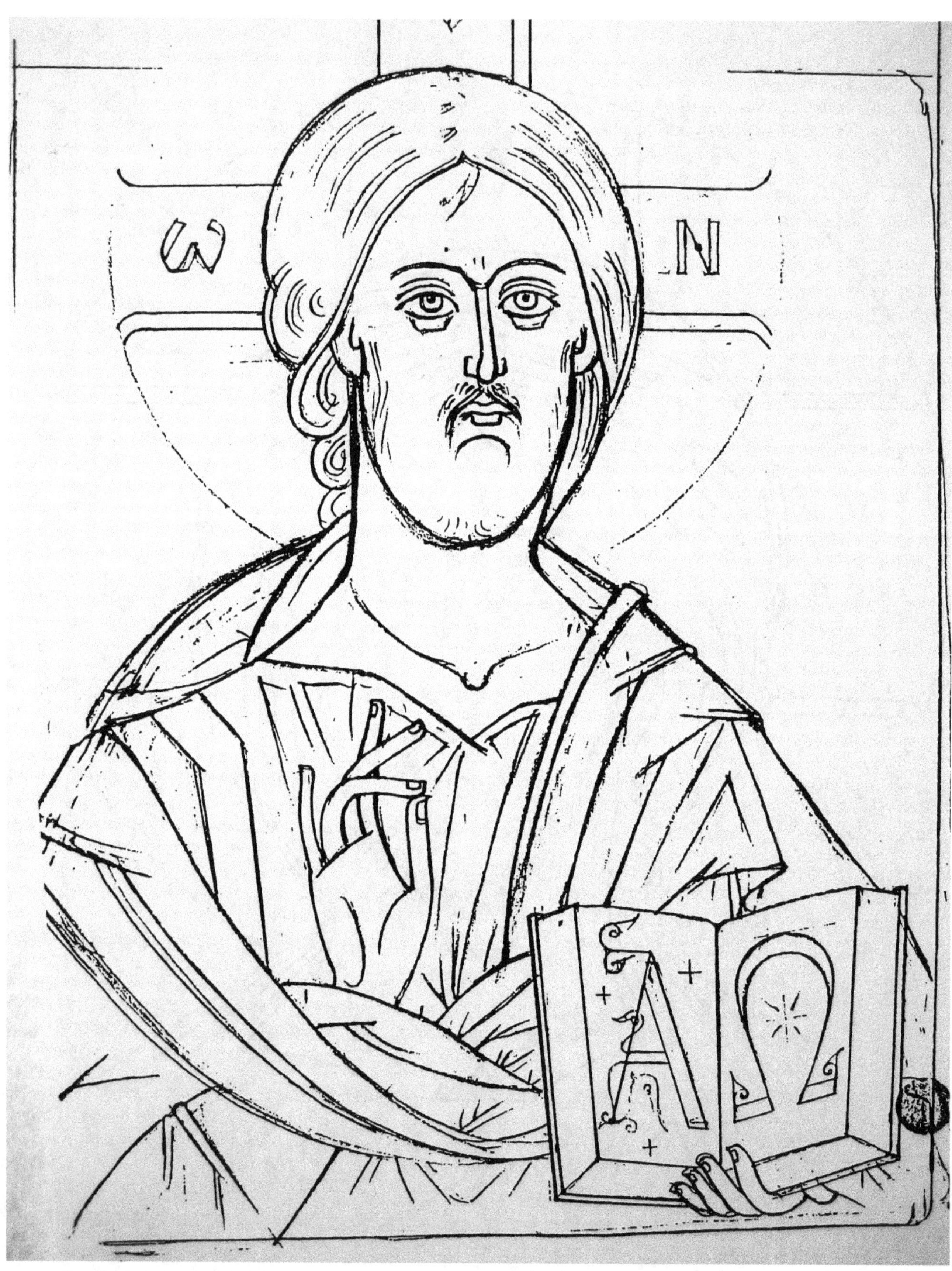

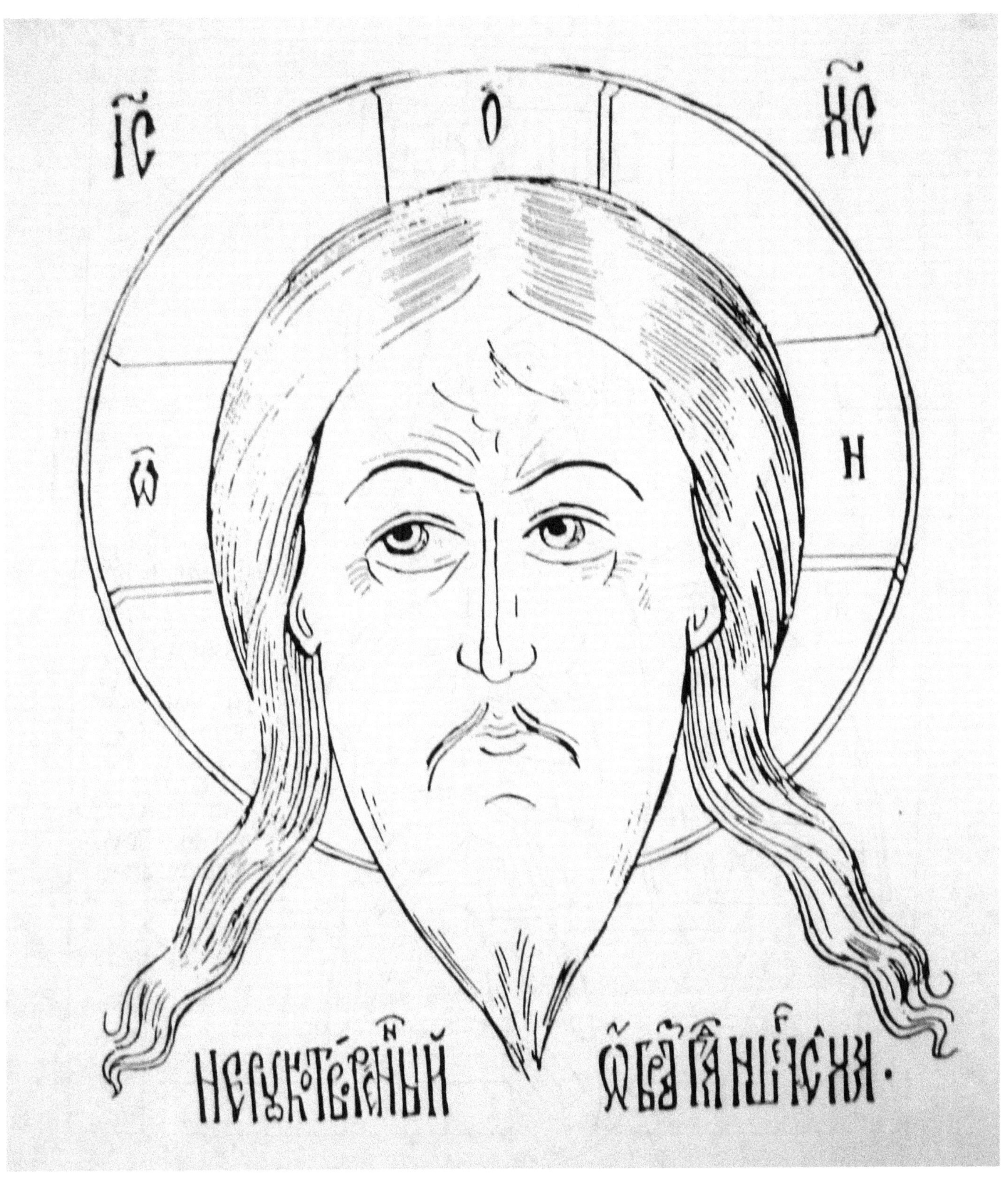
ІС ХС
О
Ѽ Н
НЕРУКОТВОРѨННЫЙ Ѿ ВОБРАЖѦ НЇ ЄГА .

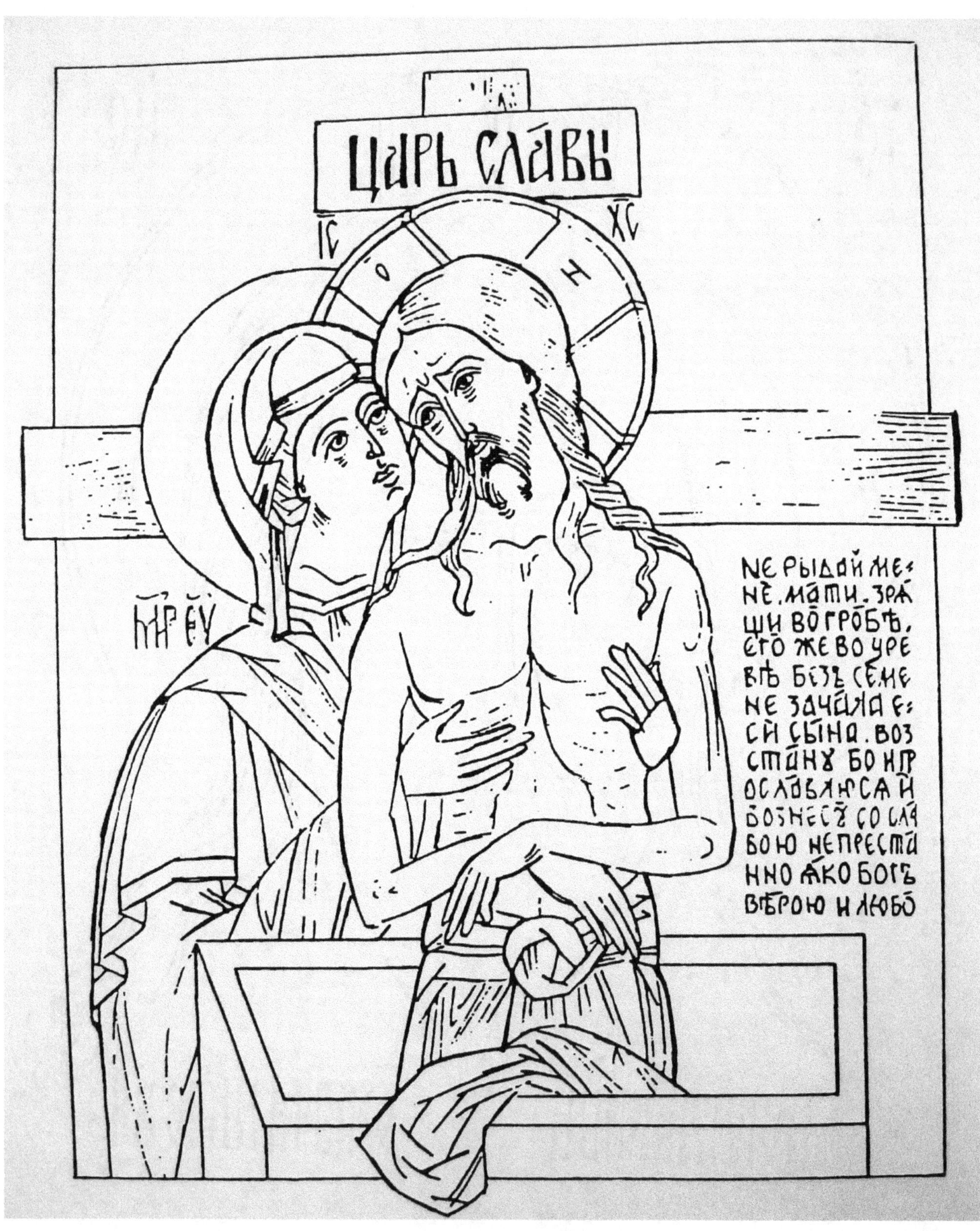
ЦАРЬ СЛАВЫ
ІС ХС
О Н
МР ѲУ
NE РЫДАЙ МЕ
НѢ. МАТИ. ЗРА
ЩИ ВО ГРОБѢ,
ЕГО ЖЕ ВО УРЕ
ВѢ БЕЗ СЕМЕ
НЕ ЗАЧАЛА Е
СИ СЫНА. ВОЗ
СТАНУ БО ИР
ОСЛАВЛЯН СА И
БОЗНЕСУ СО СЛА
БОЮ НЕПРЕСТА
НО АКО БОГЪ
ВѢРОЮ И ЛЮБО

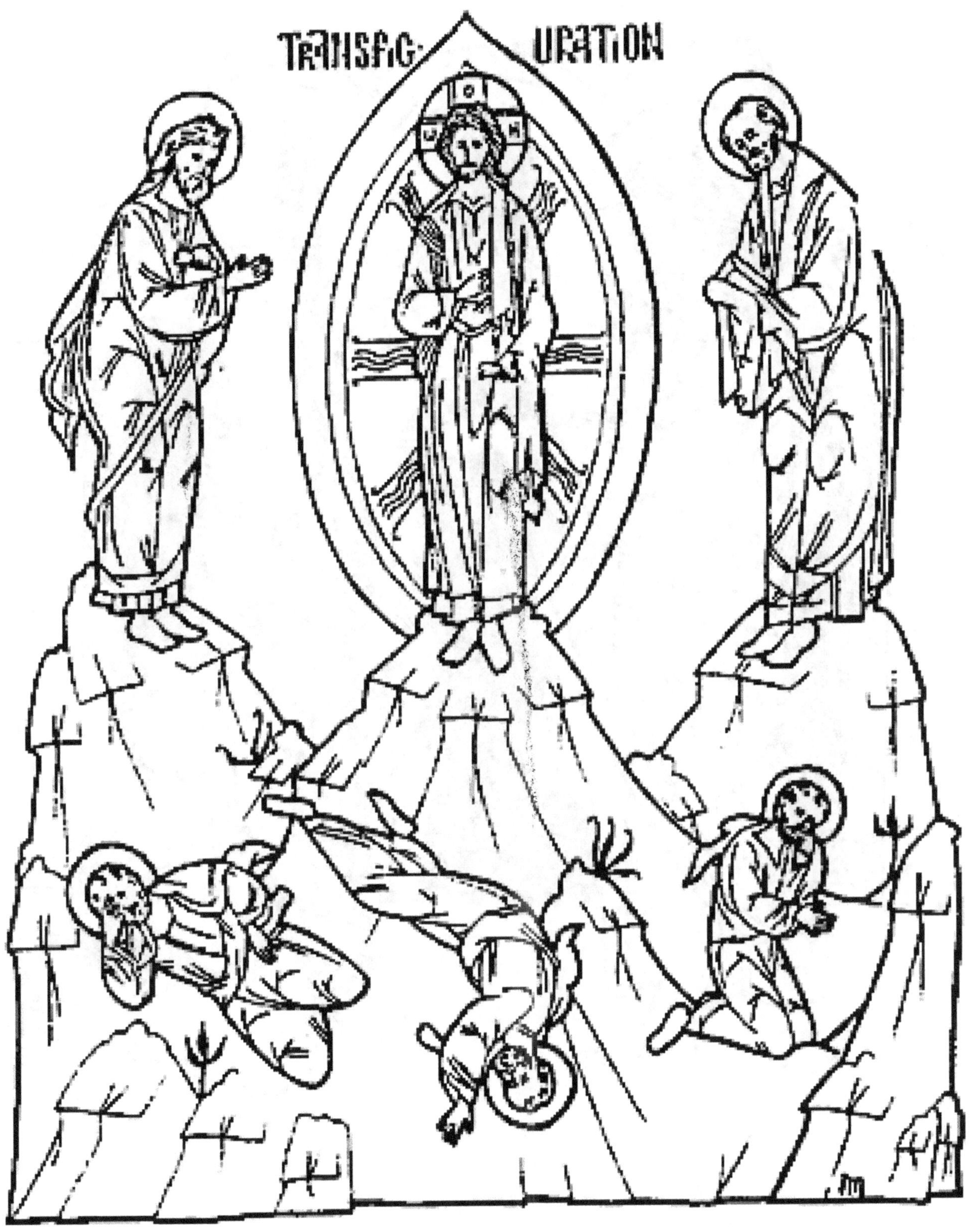
TRANSFIG URATION

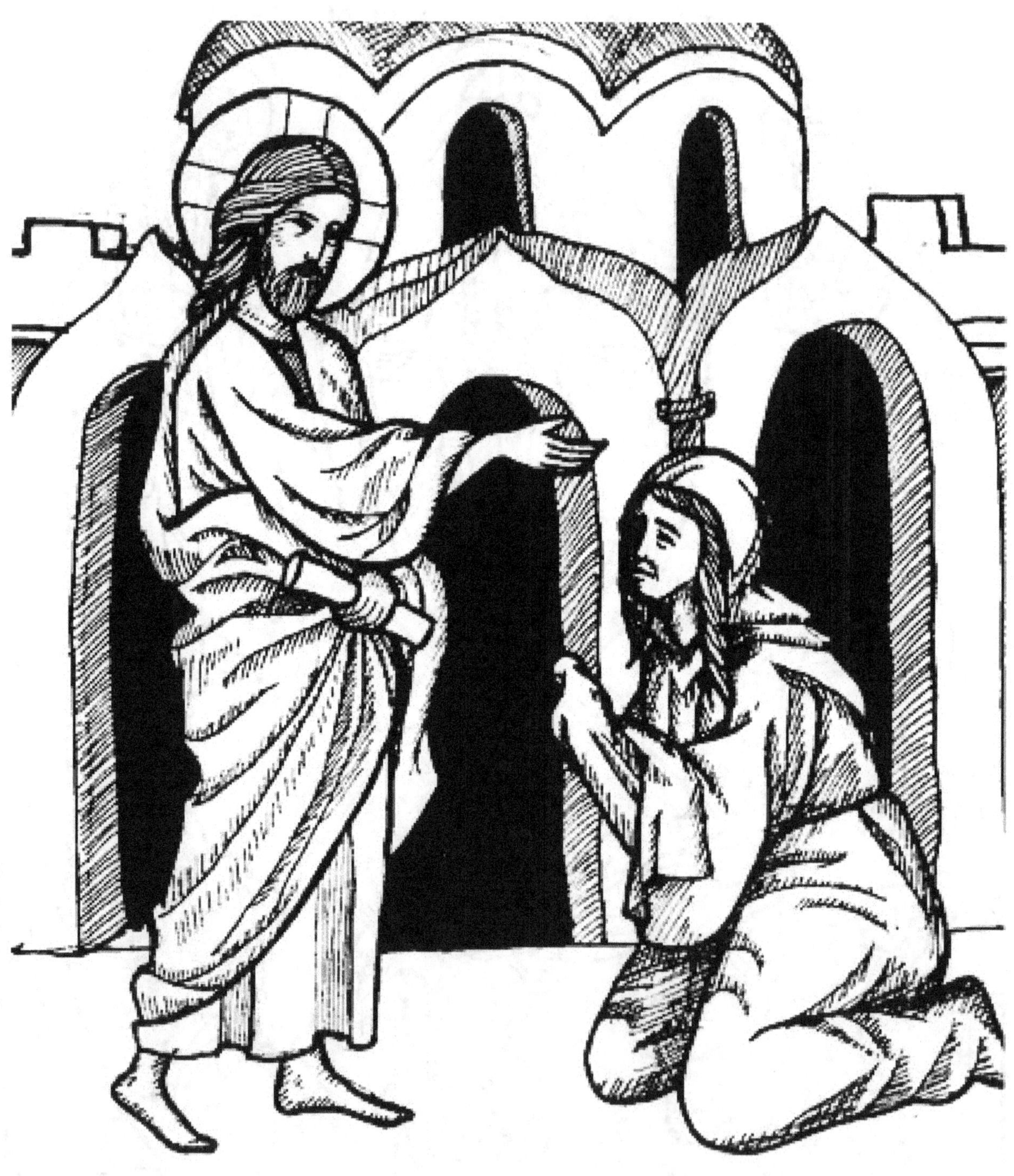

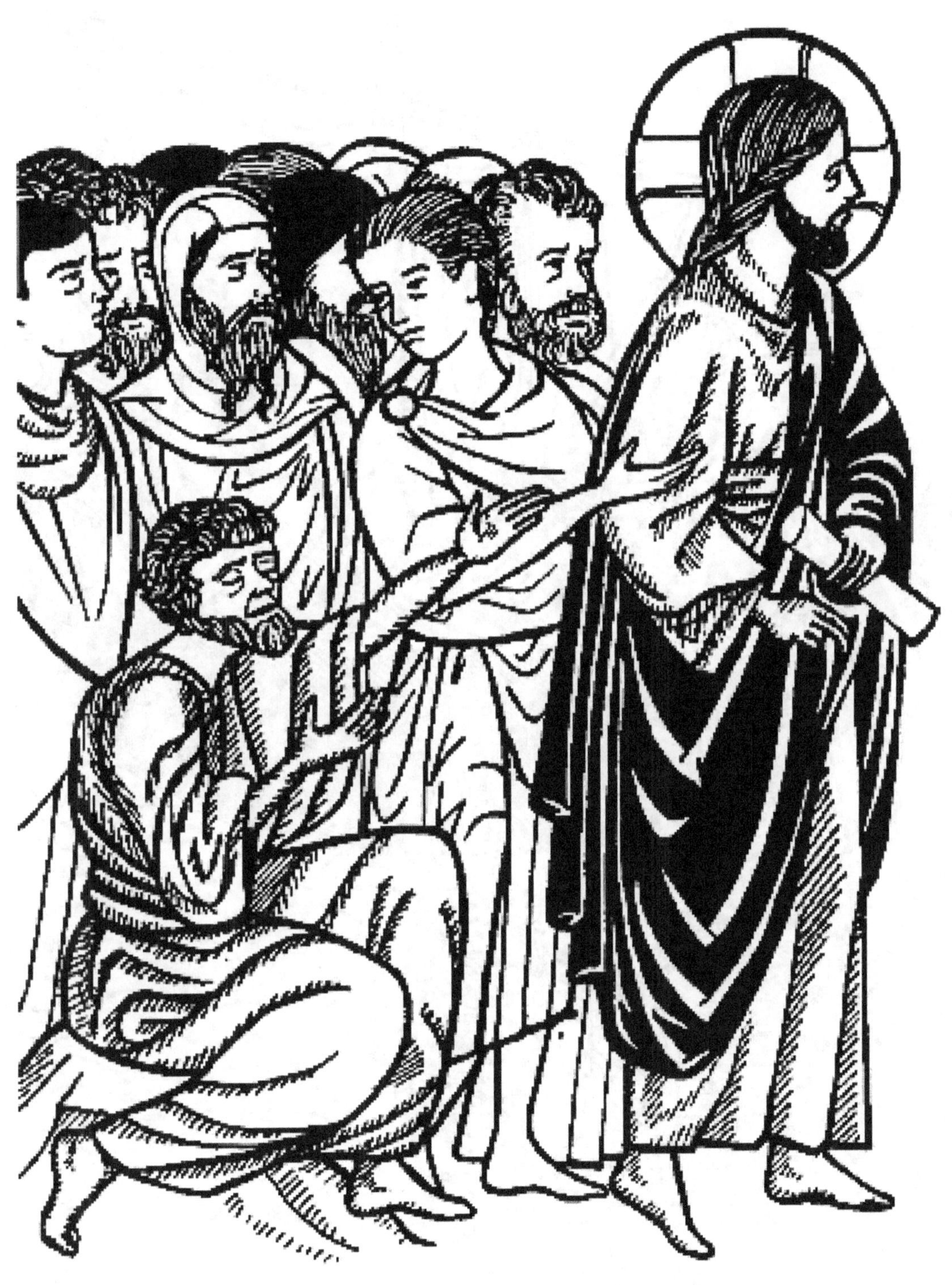

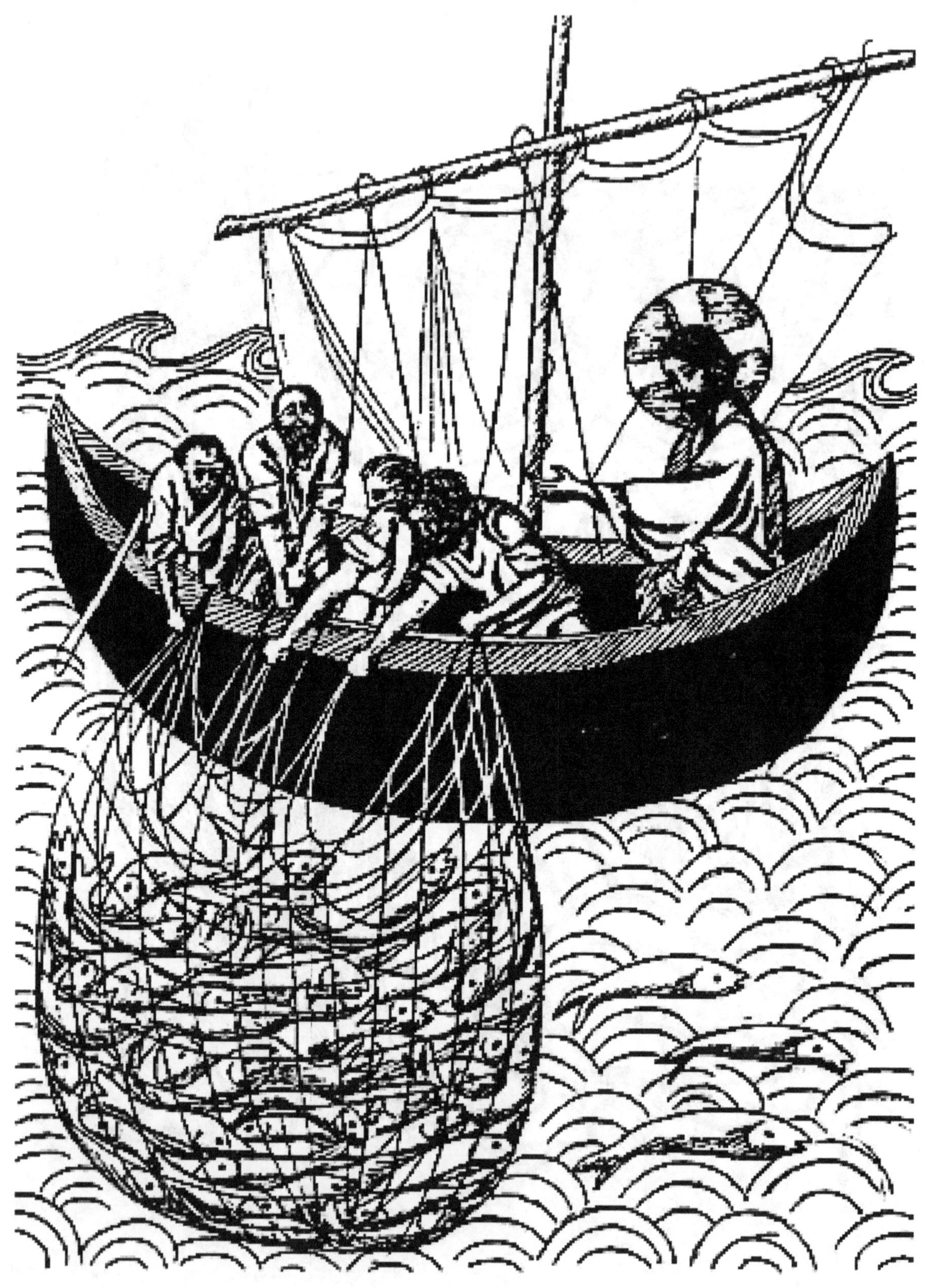

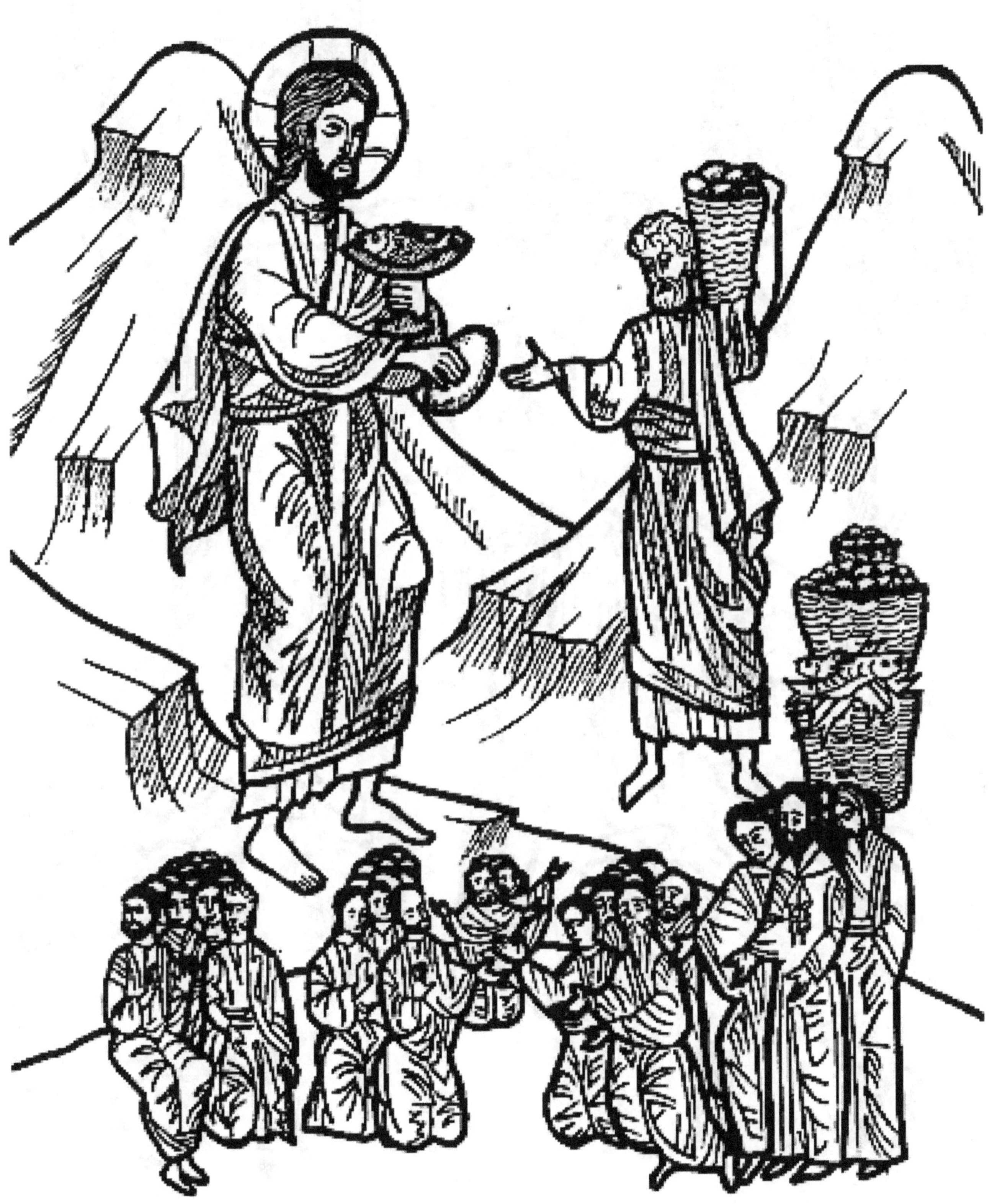

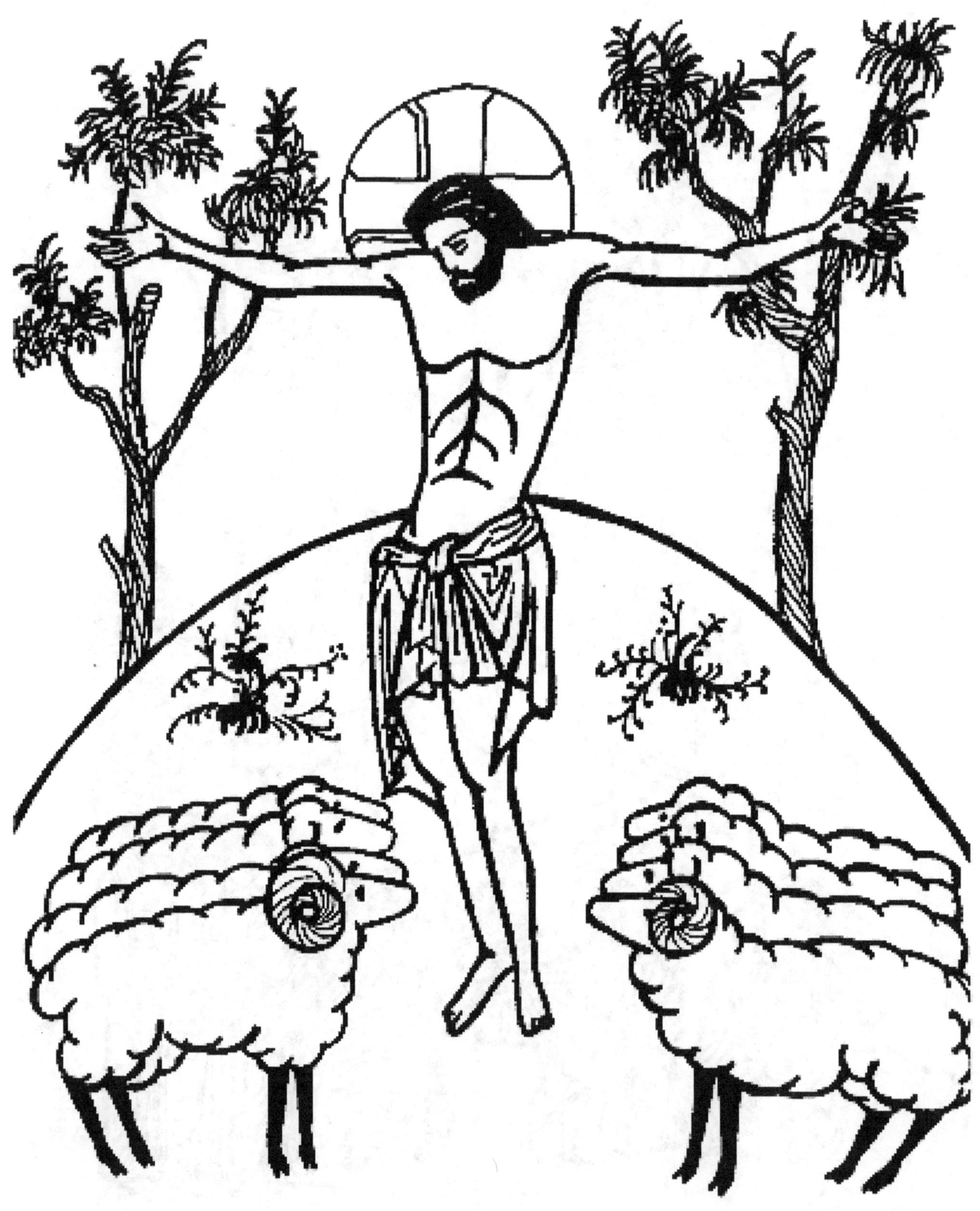

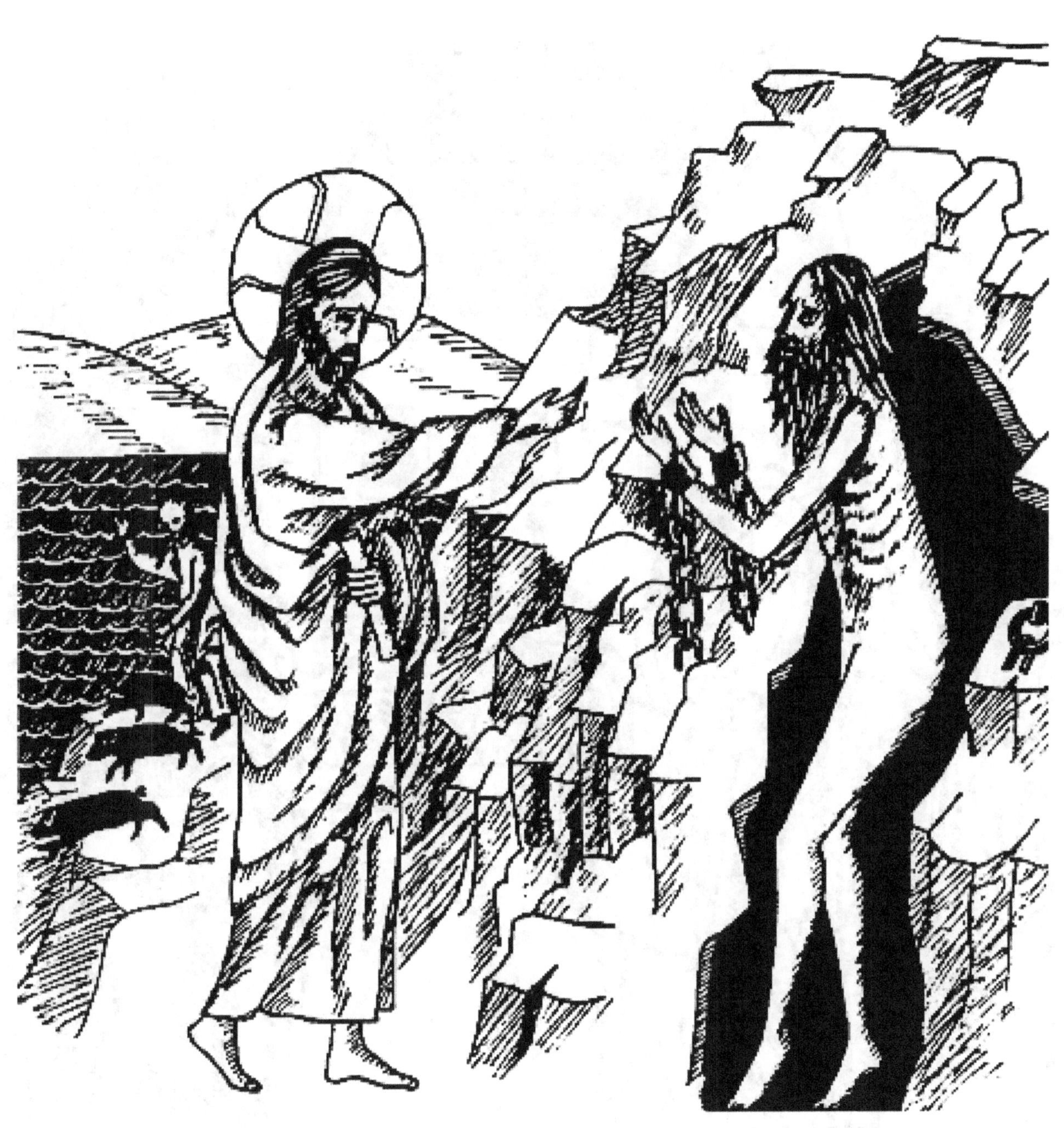

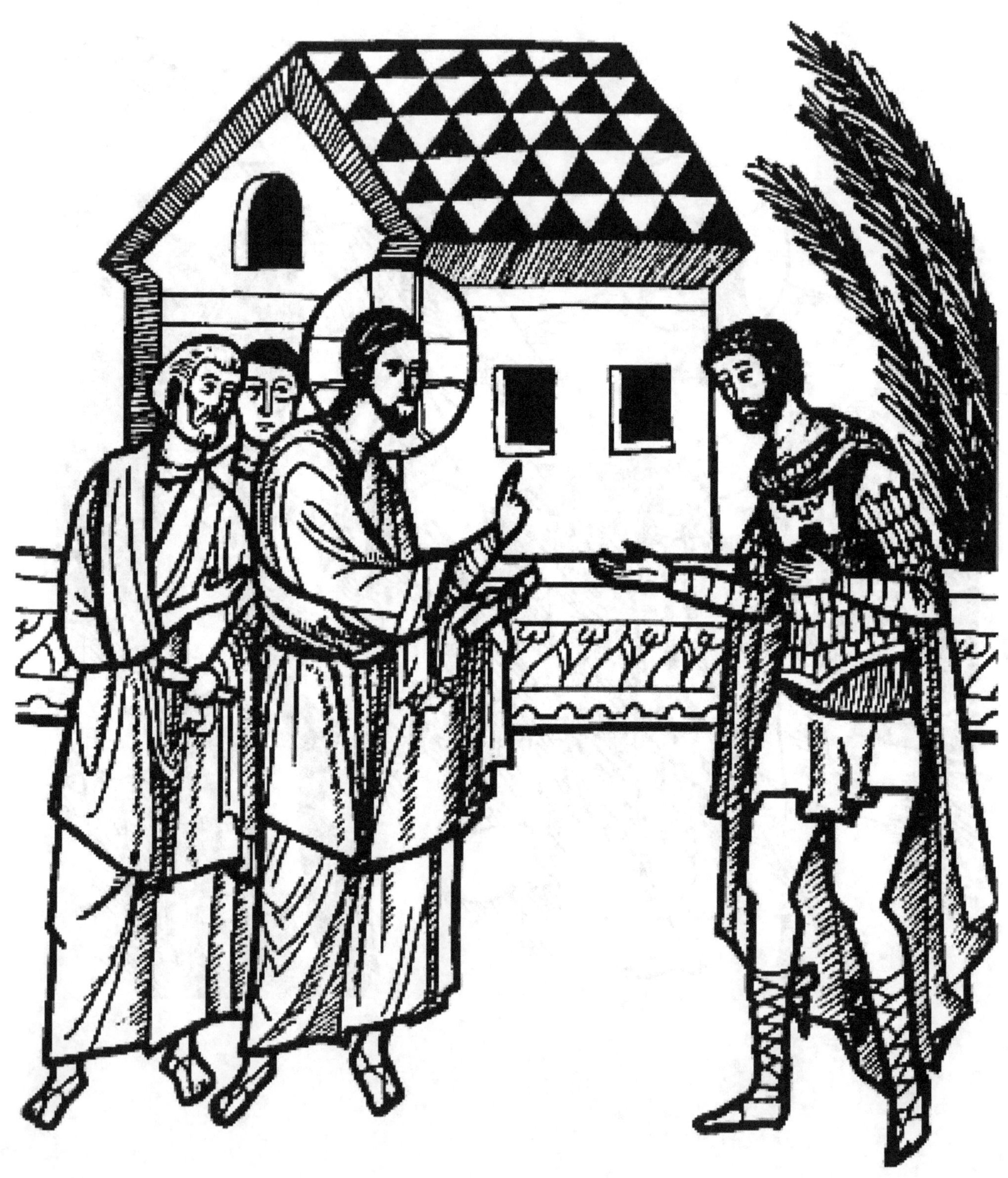

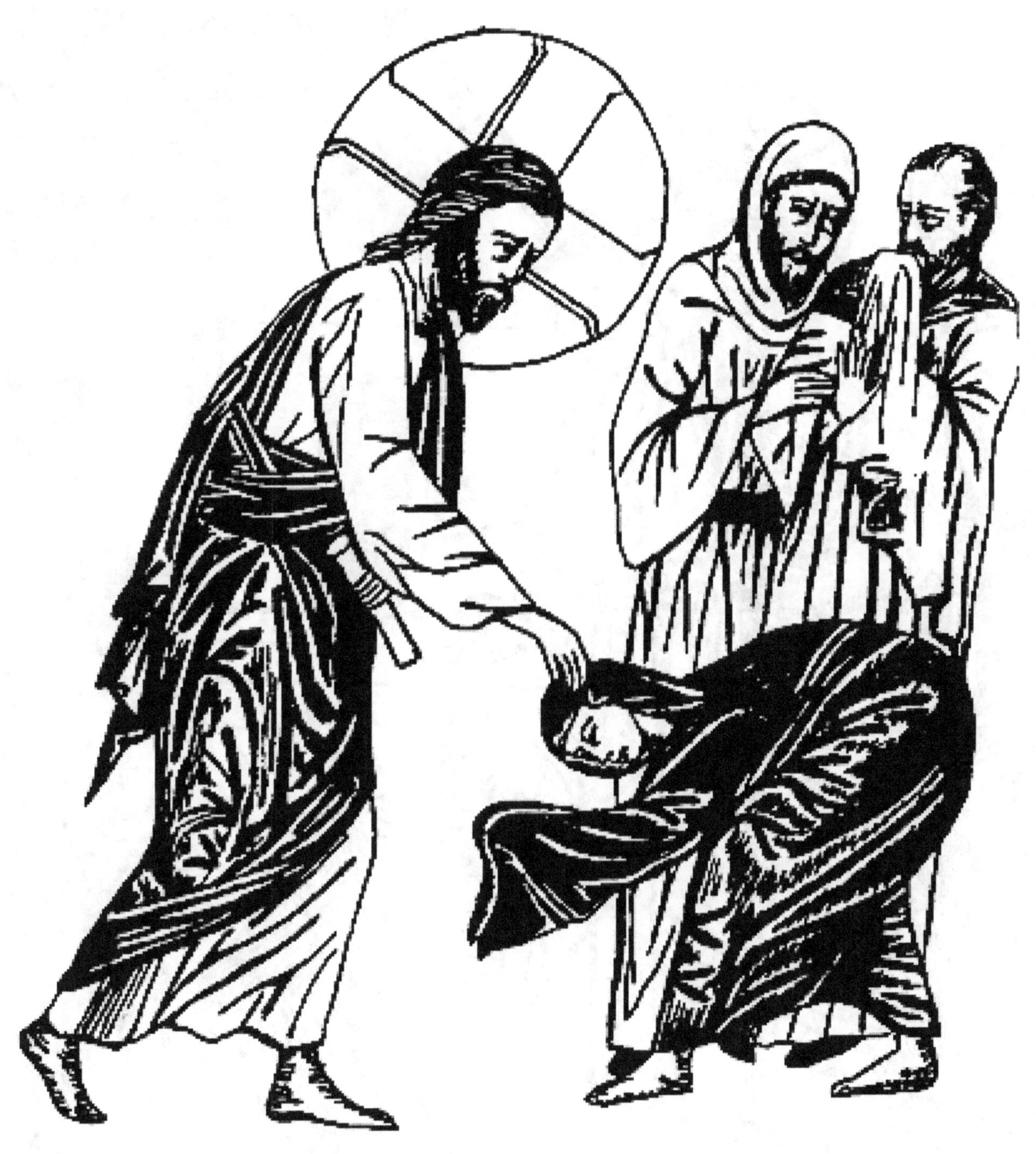

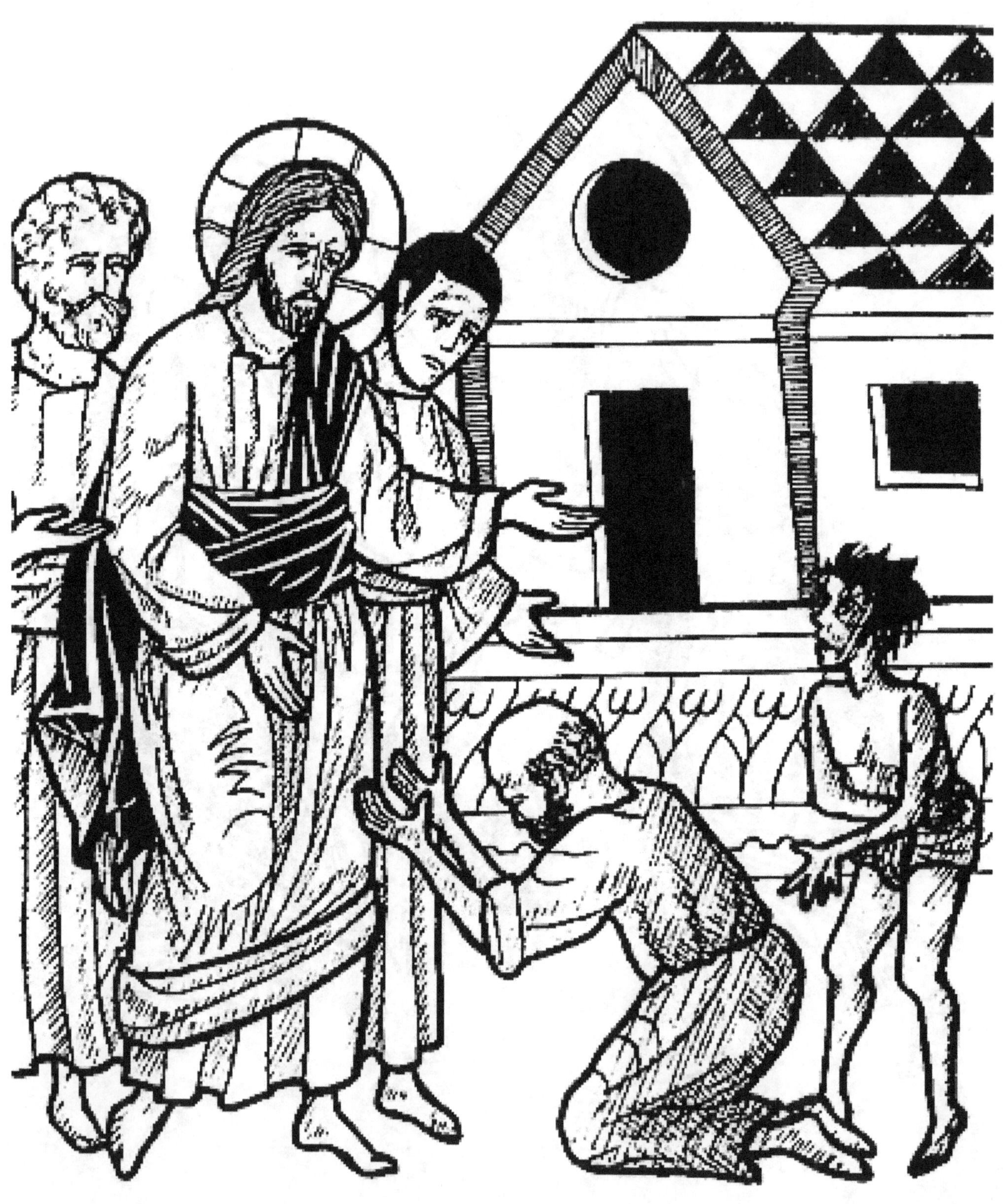

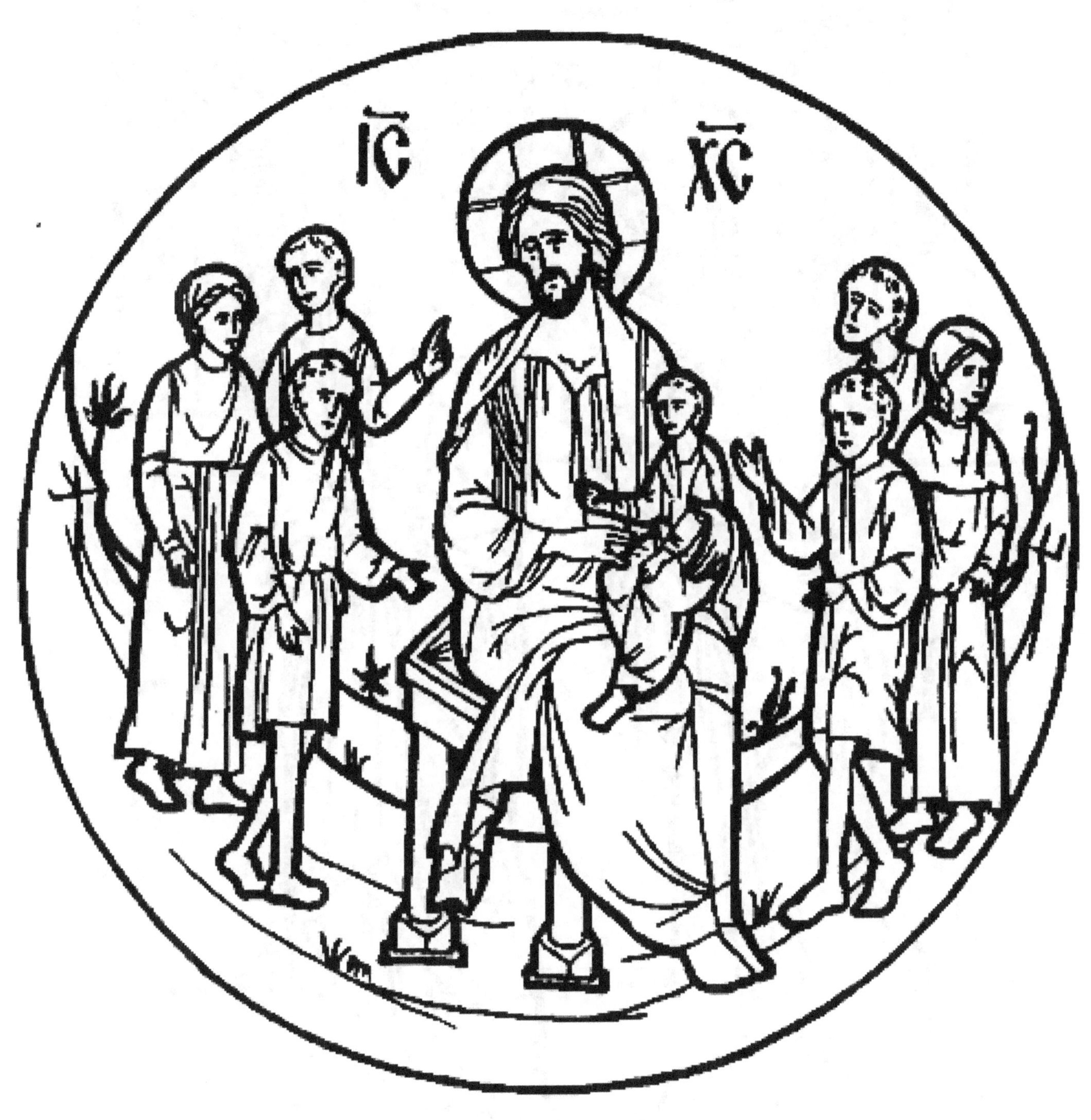
IC XC

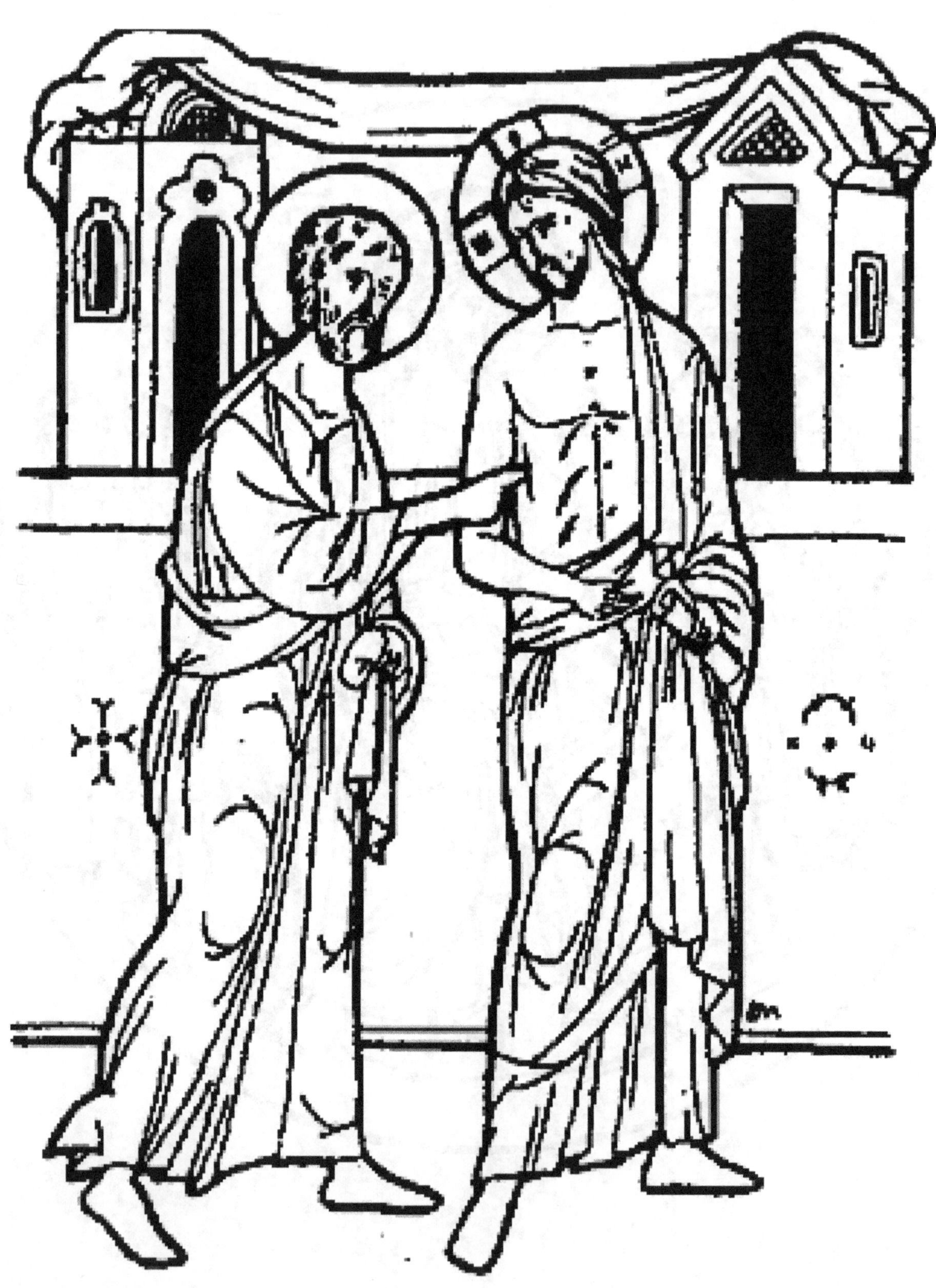

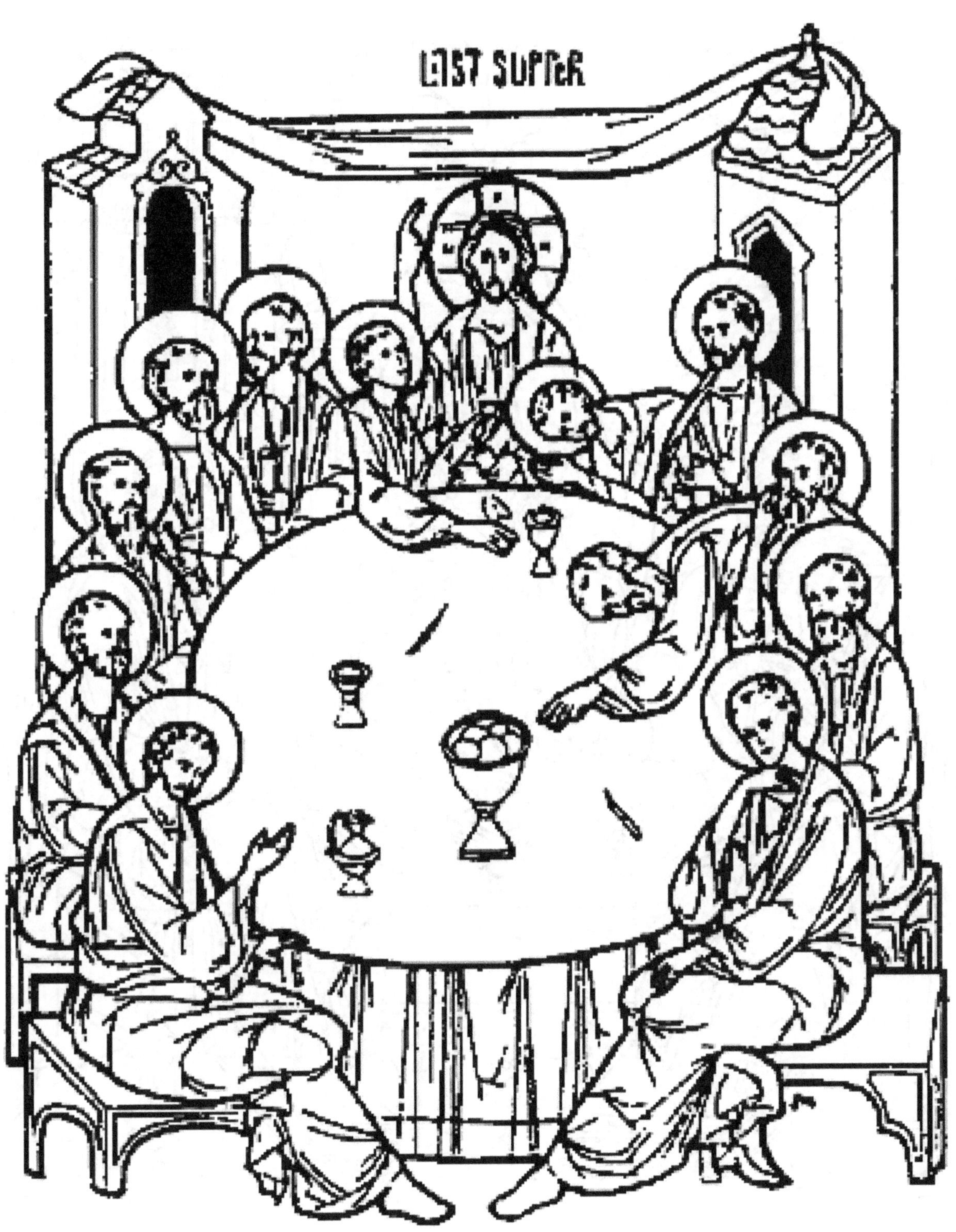
LAST SUPPER

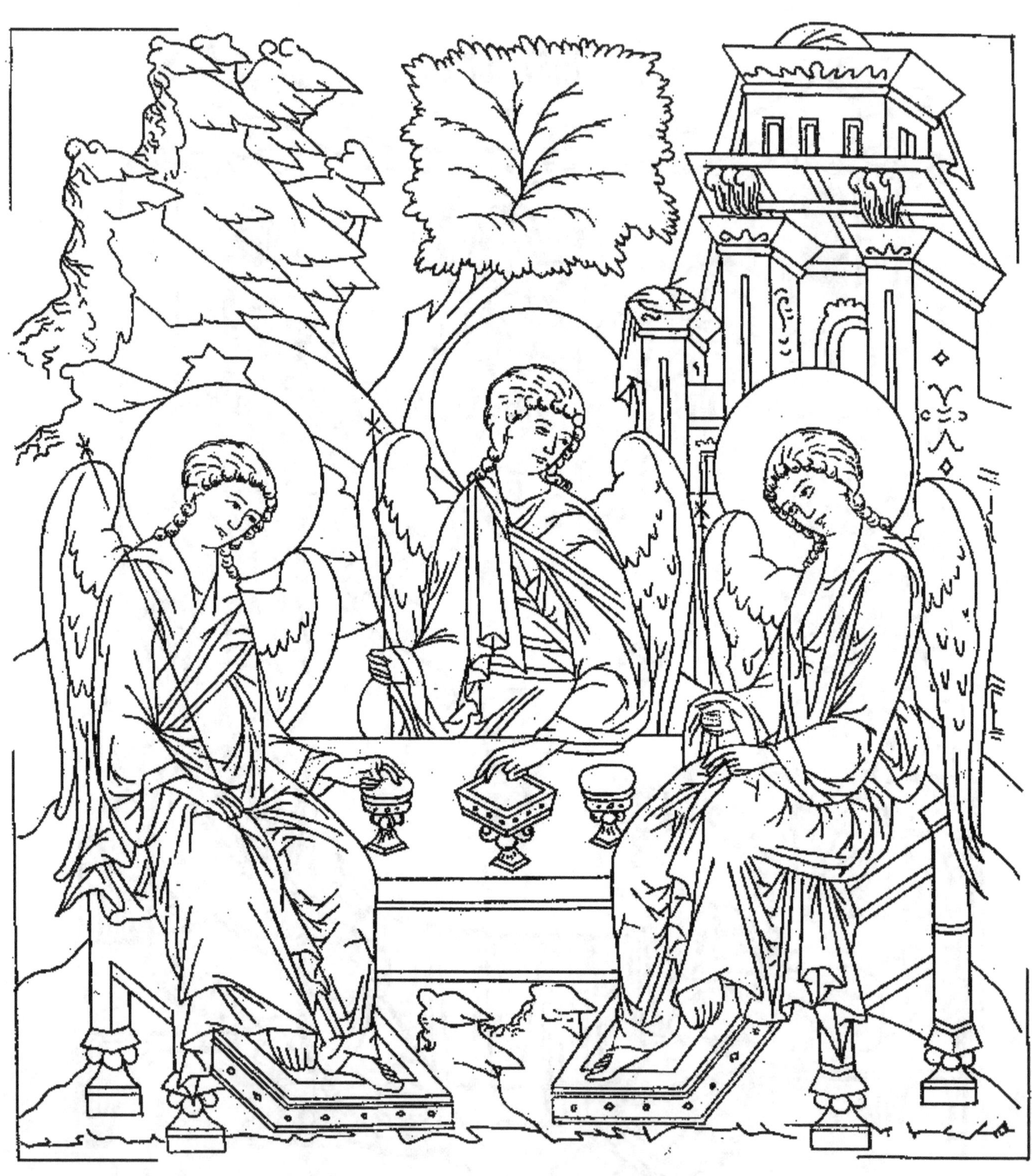

T

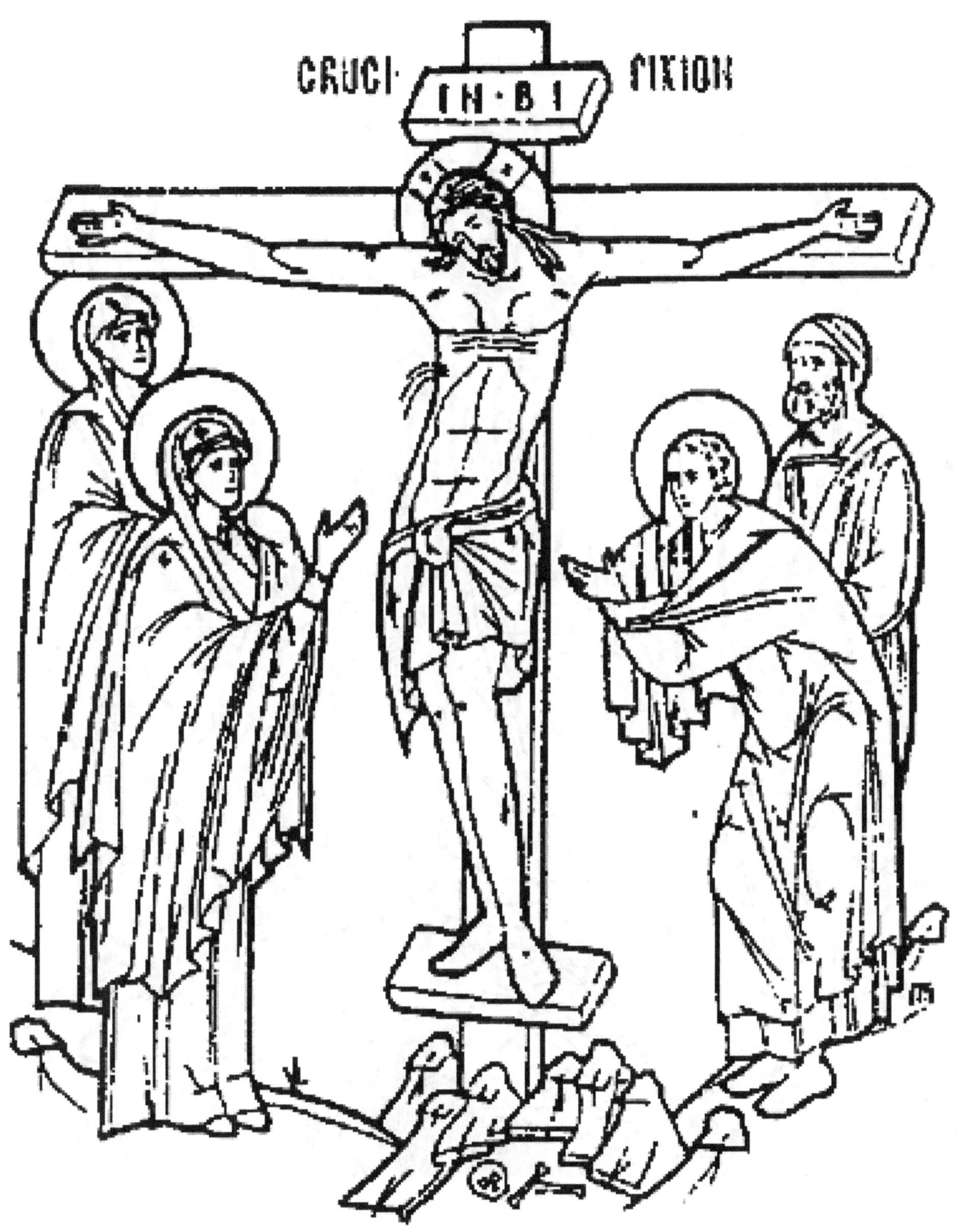

CRUCI
IXION
IN·BI

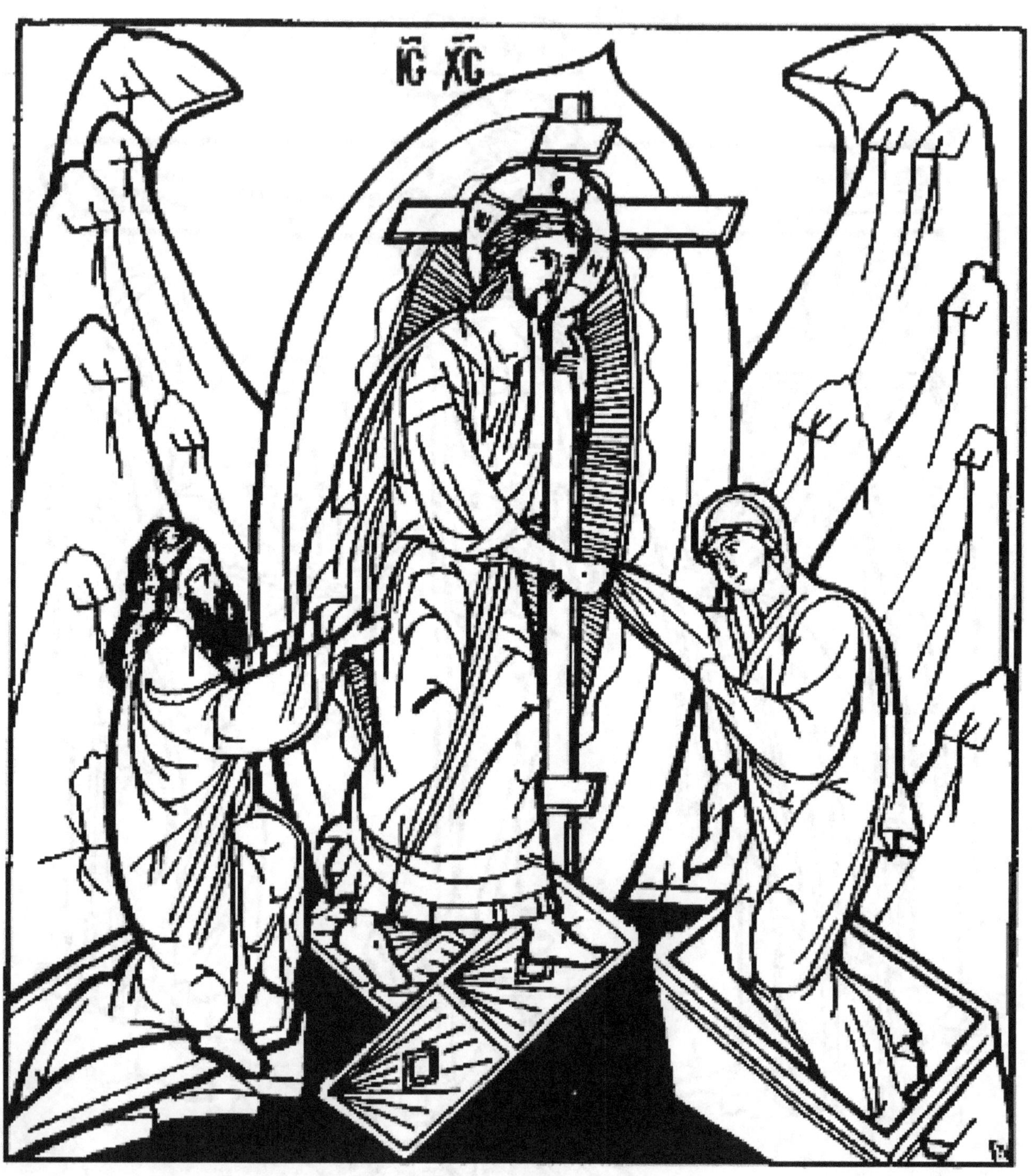
ІС ХС